MURPHY
MUST
GO!

ACKNOWLEDGEMENTS
Thanks to Sally Campbell, Kieran Allen, Shaun Harkin, Shaun
Doherty and Matt Collins for their comments on this work and to
Peter Robinson, Lina Nicolli and Mary Phillips for their work on
the production. Thanks in particular to Brian Kelly for his expert
editorial skills. And finally thanks to Wendy Ni Fhionn, for putting up
with me and all else besides. Beir Bua.

ABOUT THE AUTHOR
Seán Mitchell is a writer and socialist based in Belfast. He has
written a forthcoming book on working class unity in Belfast during
the Outdoor Relief Riots of 1932.

COVER: Portrait of James Connolly (circa 1902).
INSIDE FRONT: Boys holding up *Daily Herald* sheets reading "Murphy
Must Go" during the Dublin Lockout (*Irish Life*, October 1913).
INSIDE BACK: Making martys. General Post Office, Dublin, before its
evacuation, Easter 1916. Connolly is on the stretcher. Pádraig Pearse,
Tom Clarke and The O'Rahilly are also pictured (Walter Paget, 1918).

Published by Bookmarks Publications 2016
ISBN print edition: 978-1-910885-08-6
ISBN Kindle: 978-1-910885-09-3
ISBN ePub: 978-1-910885-10-9
ISBN PDF: 978-1-910885-11-6
Typeset by Peter Robinson
Printed by Melita Press

A Rebel's Guide to

JAMES
CONNOLLY

SEÁN MITCHELL

★ 1: INTRODUCTION

James Connolly's life and above all his execution by a British firing squad on 12 May 1916 made him a hero to Irish nationalists. His name regularly features in the long litany of great Irish historical figures cited or celebrated by some of Ireland's most conservative and reactionary forces. Streets, buildings and train stations are named after him; statues have been erected in his honour.

There is, however, another side to Connolly that Irish elites would rather you never discover: Connolly was an activist, a lifelong Marxist and a revolutionary socialist committed to the destruction of capitalism, both in Ireland and the world over. This fact alone is a source of embarrassment to an establishment in Ireland intent on claiming him as their own.

But who was James Connolly? What did he stand for? What can his life and ideas teach us today? Born in 1868 into extreme poverty, Connolly became one of the most powerful socialist orators of his generation. Along the way he was also a child labourer, a factory worker, a soldier in the British Army, a journalist and writer, and a trade union and political organiser.

His activism brought him to the very heart of some of the most iconic turn-of-the-century labour struggles—not only in Ireland, but also in Scotland and in the United States. He played an important role in some of the high points of workers' struggle in the early years of the 20th century on both sides of the Atlantic.

However, beyond his leading role as a labour agitator Connolly was also a self-educated revolutionary who understood the importance of ideas and theory. He was an avid reader and a prolific writer, publishing not only pamphlets and articles but also plays, poems and songs. He was one of the great popularisers of socialist ideas in the English language, but to communicate with immigrant workers in the US he taught himself rudimentary Italian, and was an avid student of Esperanto—the "universal language" that many radicals of his time believed would one day unite workers around the globe.

Central to his analysis, and to his efforts in all the organisations that he joined and helped found, was a commitment to the self-emancipation of workers, principled opposition to imperialism, and unwavering internationalist solidarity. His writings provide a brilliant, direct and clear exposition of the need for revolutionary socialism.

Whenever the Easter Rising is commemorated, almost every shade of political opinion in Ireland claims James Connolly as one of their own. What makes this possible is that his ideas are rarely discussed and largely ignored. This little book tries to rediscover those ideas and James Connolly's unique contributions to the international socialist movement.

★ 2: EARLY LIFE

The figure of James Connolly looms large in the pantheon of great Irish historical figures. Strange, then, that Ireland was not his place of birth. Indeed, despite a number of valiant attempts by Irish nationalist figures to suggest the contrary, the fact remains: James Connolly—Ireland's most important Marxist thinker and organiser—was born in Scotland.

Still, events in Ireland were to have a decisive impact on his life from the very beginning. Owing to the devastation imposed on the country by the Famine—or An Gorta Mór (The Great Hunger)—millions of Irish people either starved or emigrated. Those who could afford to set off for lands afar; Australia, New Zealand and of course North America being the most common destinations. Those who could not afford the trip were forced to look closer to home, moving in their thousands into the working class districts of industrial Britain. John and Mary Connolly—two Irish immigrants from County Monaghan, who moved to Scotland in search of work—were part of this mass migration.

The Connollys settled in the impoverished district of Cowgate in Edinburgh, known locally as "little Ireland" because of its large immigrant population. Cowgate was a slum in the strictest sense of the word. Here immigrants crammed into small, poorly sanitised, single-room dwellings. Each tiny room in the area housed on average seven people. It was within the walls of these cramped conditions that Mary and John raised a family and in 1868 they had their third son, James Connolly.

Connolly had a tough upbringing. Like most children of Irish immigrants, he attended a Catholic primary school, St Patrick's. His formal education did not last long unfortunately and at the tender age of 11 he left school and started his life as a child labourer. His first job was working at menial tasks—cleaning print rollers and doing odd jobs for management—at the *Edinburgh Evening News*. A factory inspector would later dismiss him from his job because of his age (despite the fact he was told to stand on a box that made him look taller). Money, however, was desperately scarce at home and the young Connolly was forced to seek new employment. Landing a job as a baker's apprentice at the age of 12, he worked from six in the morning until late at night. Years later he told his daughter Nora that he would often pray that he would find the place burnt down when he returned the next day.

Work at the bread factory proved to be a punishing experience for Connolly. He was still only a young boy and his health suffered greatly as a result. Again forced to seek work elsewhere, he laboured for about a year in a small mosaic factory in less noxious circumstances. Here Connolly's life took an unexpected, even unusual, turn. At 14 he falsified his age in order to enlist in the Royal Scots Regiment. Little is known about Connolly's time in the British Army, though we do know that it was in the service of Queen Victoria that he first set foot in Ireland, stationed first in the Curragh Military Camp in County Kildare and later in the capital city, Dublin. It was during this time that he met Lillie Reynolds, later his wife and lifelong partner.

Connolly rarely spoke of his time in the military, but it's not hard to imagine that this experience had a profound impact on the anti-imperialist politics he would come to adopt. Years later, in his paper the *Workers' Republic*, he described the British Army as a "moral cesspool corrupting all within its bounds" (*Workers' Republic*, 15 July 1899). He was no doubt thinking of his own past.

Connolly spent seven years in the British Army, but when his battalion was redeployed to India he went AWOL, returning to Scotland to live with his brother in Dundee. It was during this period that he first got involved in the socialist movement. Scotland was then in the grip of "new unionism"—marked by a steep rise in class conflict that saw a massive upsurge in trade union membership and strike activity. In Dundee there were huge demonstrations, some numbering tens of thousands, against a ban on public processions. Connolly's older brother John was heavily involved in the upheaval and was subsequently sacked for organising a march in the city.

Many of the demonstrations were organised by the Socialist League, a split from the Social Democratic Federation (SDF), one of the earliest Marxist groups in Britain. Connolly joined the group and became an active socialist. The left in Scotland at this time was small, isolated and divided into a number of different groups whose memberships often overlapped. Connolly was a member of, or had associations with, most of these groups at one point or another. By the time he left Scotland in 1896, for example, he was the secretary of the Scottish Socialist Federation and the Scottish Labour Party.

Circumstance would eventually force Connolly to leave Scotland. But his time there had a profound impact on his political outlook. It is our experiences in life that make us who we are. And James Connolly was a product of his environment like everyone else is. But it was also this experience that led him to want to change the world around him. His upbringing in abject poverty, his time as a child labourer and his first-hand experience of military life set him on a path that would lead him to the politics of socialism and anti-imperialism and to a return to Ireland.

★ 3: THE IRISH SOCIALIST REPUBLICAN PARTY

Out of work and languishing in poverty, in December 1895, James Connolly placed a small advert in a socialist paper offering his services as an organiser. He received a single solitary reply from a tiny left wing group in Ireland—the Dublin Socialist Club—offering him a post as full-time organiser. Connolly jumped at the chance and accepted the offer, immigrating with his growing family to Ireland the following May. He brought little with him except his prized collection of books and pamphlets, impressive for a man of such modest means. He was to be paid a pound a week for his services, though he rarely received the full amount and was often forced to seek work to supplement his income.

Still, Connolly was to have a considerable impact on the development of the turn-of-the-century left in Ireland. One of his first actions was to suggest to his new comrades that the Dublin Socialist Club should be disbanded. And on 29 May 1896 they did just that, reconstituting themselves as the Irish Socialist Republican Party (ISRP), Ireland's first revolutionary Marxist party. Their motto was the slogan of the French revolutionary

Camille Desmoulins: "The great appear great to us only because we are on our knees: Let us rise."

The party first came to prominence in 1897 during the "Diamond Jubilee" of Queen Victoria. Connolly and the ISRP used the event to highlight the brutality of the British Empire and in collaboration with Maud Gonne—the renowned feminist and republican—they organised a series of public protests. A mock funeral procession was arranged with Connolly and his comrades carrying a coffin with the words "British Empire" emblazoned on its side. Later, when the police blocked the procession, Connolly threw the coffin into the River Liffey, declaring, "Here goes the coffin of the British Empire", an act that resulted in him being arrested (Donal Nevin, *James Connolly: A Full Life*, 2006, p88). The party would also organise high-profile demonstrations against the visit of the Duke and Duchess of York and against the Boer War.

Connolly was undoubtedly the driving force behind the ISRP. He shaped the routines of the organisation around those he had learned while active in Scotland. In addition to being the party's sole organiser, he was also its chief orator, lecturing on a wide range of subjects including Socialism and Strikes, Socialism and Nationalism, Socialism and State Capitalism, and the Paris Commune. In the warmer months of summer the party held open air meetings, some attracting in excess of 200 people. And when the cold air of winter descended, they would revert to a routine of indoor lectures or reading groups on socialist literature.

Central to the ISRP's activity was its newspaper, the *Workers' Republic*. Connolly borrowed £50 from the legendary Scottish labour figure Keir Hardie to launch the paper. Despite this, *Workers' Republic* was beset with financial difficulties from the outset and publication was at times intermittent. Nevertheless, the paper was crucial to the routines of the ISRP and to building a base of support for socialist ideas. Connolly wrote regularly for the paper on a number of different topics. There was no doubting the strength of his prose: sharp, illuminating and often humorous. He had a gift for popularising ideas in a way that was accessible and attractive to his working class readership.

The party also sought to promote its ideas in the electoral arena and Connolly and the ISRP stood on a number of occasions. That said, however, they were far from an electoralist party. As Connolly said, "The election of a Socialist to any public body at present is only valuable in so far as it is the return of a disturber of the political peace" (*Labour Chronicle*, 1 December 1894). Elections could be used as a platform for socialist ideas, he argued, but they were not the be-all and end-all.

The party also produced a political programme outlining its demands. It contained a number of proposals common to the international socialist movement at the time: the nationalisation of railways, the establishment of state banks, free education and universal suffrage, to name a few. This was not the end of the ISRP's ambitions, however. Connolly wanted to create a truly democratic socialism in Ireland where the wealth and economy of the nation were in the control of its people. It was not simply a case of the state nationalising sectors of the economy: workers themselves would also have to own and run them democratically. "Socialism" he wrote "implies above all things the co-operative control by the workers of the machinery of production; without this co-operative control the public ownership by the State is not Socialism—it is only State Capitalism" (*Workers' Republic*, 10 June 1899).

It was the party's approach to the National Question in Ireland, however, that broke new ground. Connolly and the ISRP were committed opponents of imperialism in Ireland and supported the demand for an independent Ireland. However, they were not content to limit themselves to either a form of Home Rule (espoused by moderate nationalists), or even an Irish Republic (advocated by more militant republicans). Ireland's national subjugation was a direct consequence of capitalism, Connolly argued; the real demands of the Irish people could only be met by a complete overhaul of society, by the creation of a socialist society. He pointed to the example of the US. There a republic had been long established and British rule broken only to be replaced by a "power of the purse [that] has established a new tyranny under the forms of freedom". Connolly warned that a similar fate would befall an Irish Republic if it did not break from the shackles of capitalism. "If you remove the English army to-morrow and hoist the green flag over Dublin Castle," he insisted, "unless you set about the organisation of the Socialist Republic your efforts would be in vain" (*Shan Van Vocht*, January 1897).

Connolly worked with militant republicans for much of his political life, and sought to win them to a socialist position. However, he criticised the "ridiculous secrecy" of the movement and argued that only the force of the working class was capable of "the revolutionary reconstruction of society and the incidental destruction of the British Empire" (James Connolly, *Erin's Hope, the End and the Means*, 1909).

Connolly's opposition to physical force republicanism, however, did not stem from passivism. Instead it came from his desire to include the masses in the struggle: "If the time should arrive when the party of progress finds its way to freedom barred...if it has exhausted all the peaceful means at its disposal for the purpose of demonstrating to the people and their enemies that the new revolutionary ideas do possess the suffrage of the majority; then, but not till then, the party which represents the revolutionary idea is justified in taking steps to assume the powers of government, and in using the weapons of force to dislodge the usurping class or government in possession" (James Connolly, *Erin's Hope, the End and the Means*).

Connolly's criticism of the tactics of republicanism did not mean that he absented himself from struggles against national oppression. His approach to the Irish language is illuminating in this regard. During this period Ireland was undergoing a "Gaelic revival". Thousands of people, particularly the country's more progressive intellectuals, were rediscovering Irish culture and language after years of suppression by the British. Connolly and the ISRP were supportive of this movement, but argued that its aims could only be met by a socialist transformation of society. "The chief enemy of a Celtic revival today", argued Connolly, "is the crushing force of capitalism" (*Workers' Republic*, 1 October 1898).

That said, Connolly was disdainful of mystical nationalism. Like many socialist internationalists of his time, he foresaw the gradual emergence of a common world language, believing, he wrote, "in the necessity, and indeed in the inevitability of a universal language". This emerging unity of peoples of different nationalities, however, would not "be brought about, or even hastened, by smaller races or nations consenting to the extinction of their language" (*Workers' Republic*, 1 October 1898). Indeed his position was not restricted to the Irish language. During one election campaign the ISRP produced a leaflet in Yiddish, the main language of the small Jewish community in Dublin at the time who like Jews elsewhere across Europe were often victims of anti-Semitism.

The ISRP made an important political contribution to the development of the left in Ireland, but it was modest in size and its membership never exceeded 100. The poor financial state of the party increasingly forced Connolly to seek employment elsewhere. This and his dire financial situation at home convinced Connolly that he had to emigrate once more. He stayed for a time in Scotland but then decided on a move farther ashore. And in 1903 his journey took another twist as he set off for the US.

from under the Socialist Trade and Labour Alliance"
(James Connolly, Daniel DeLeon, *The Connolly-DeLeon
Controversy*, 1904).

Connolly argued that this orientation left the SLP
unable "to take a real live part in the struggles of the
workers", confining it to expounding meaningless slogans
and abstract propaganda: "I stated that such theories
destroy the fighting power of the Socialist Trade and
Labour Alliance as a bona fide trade union; or to quote
my words literally, made it a mere ward healing club for
the SLP... Imagine a trade union which would fight against
a reduction of wages, but prevented from fighting for a
rise, because taught by its organisers that a rise was no
good. What a picnic the employers would have! Every
reduction they could enforce would be a permanent one,
as our principles would forbid us demanding a rise, it
being no benefit" (James Connolly, Daniel DeLeon, *The
Connolly-DeLeon Controversy*).

Connolly wiped the floor with De Leon on the question of wages and strikes. But he was on shakier ground
over the question of religion. Connolly believed that
the SLP position on religion was too dogmatic, arguing
that it created unnecessary barriers between the party
and those workers influenced by religion. Certainly,
Connolly was correct to call out the SLP over its crude
anti-clericalism. After all, as Lenin argued: "unity in this
really revolutionary struggle of the oppressed class for
the creation of a paradise on Earth is more important
to us than unity of proletarian opinion on paradise in
heaven" (V I Lenin, *Socialism and Religion*, 3 December
1905). Furthermore, Connolly understood that in the
atmosphere of anti-Catholicism then being directed at

immigrants from an Irish or Italian background, it was important for revolutionaries not only to distinguish themselves from the anti-immigrant demagogues—who attempted to justify their prejudice by pointing to the "foreign" religious practices of ordinary immigrants—but also to fight to win these sections of the working class to the SLP.

In his argument with De Leon, however, Connolly made a number of unnecessary concessions that would have weakened rather than strengthened the revolutionary movement. In particular, he at times underestimated how family structures could be used to strengthen the hierarchical relation that suited capitalism and underpinned women's oppression. Though shaped by many conservative notions common in his day, Connolly's position on the oppression of women was still far more advanced than most radicals at the time: "The worker is the slave of capitalist society, the female worker is the slave of that slave... In its march towards freedom, the working class of Ireland must cheer on the efforts of those women who, feeling on their souls and bodies the fetters of the ages, have arisen to strike them off, and cheer all the louder if in its hatred of thraldom and passion for freedom the women's army forges ahead of the militant army of Labour" (James Connolly, *The Re-Conquest of Ireland*, 1915).

Connolly's experience in the SLP shaped his views on political organisation. Indeed much of the ISRP's approach to propaganda and trade unionism in Ireland had been modelled on the SLP. However he grew tired of the SLP's sectarian approach to working class struggle and increasingly began to focus on his trade union activism. He worked for a time as an insurance salesman and in other temporary jobs but it took him some time before he could to save enough to rent a house and send off tickets for Lillie and the children. By the summer of 1904 they were all set to sail and join him.

Connolly looked forward eagerly to being reunited with Lillie and their seven children, but disaster would strike before their arrival. Their first-born daughter, Mona, was anxious with anticipation: "This time tomorrow we will be on the high seas on our way out to Father," she told her sister Ina. "Will he think I've grown big?" Tragically, she would never find out. During a visit to her aunt's house, on the eve of their departure for the US, Mona was the victim of a horrific accident, in which her apron caught fire, engulfing her in flames. She died the next day of her burns, aged just 13. In death as in life, the effects of poverty follow the poor, and the Connolly family were no different. Mona was buried in an unmarked "paupers' grave" and the family were unable to attend her funeral due to the cost of missing the boat for the US. There is no telling the grief that Connolly would have felt when he counted six rather than seven children by Lillie's side when they arrived (see Lorcan Collins, *James Connolly: 16 Lives*, pp128-132).

And yet he trundled on, through struggles great and small. The "Rebel Girl" Elizabeth Gurley Flynn, the great American socialist labour leader, remembered it a "pathetic sight to see [Connolly] standing, poorly clad, at the door of Cooper Union or some other East Side hall, selling his little paper." "None of the prosperous professional Irish", she recalled, "lent him a helping hand at that time." Not for lack of a philanthropic spirit, of course, did his fellow countrymen ignore him. "Connolly was anathema to them", said Flynn, "because he was a 'Socialist'" (Elizabeth Gurley Flynn, *The Rebel Girl*, 1979).

★ 5: THE INDUSTRIAL WORKERS OF THE WORLD

Connolly was at the centre of the growth of a very significant organisation in the history of the labour movement, the Industrial Workers of the World (IWW).

The IWW had its origins in the Colorado Labour Wars of 1903-04—a period of intense industrial conflict between the Western Federation of Miners and local capitalists. The strike had been intense, but was ultimately defeated by the failure of the American Federation of Labor (AFL) to call out its members in solidarity with the action. This capitulation—as well as the experience of the Russian Revolution in 1905—inspired a number of labour figures to pursue a more militant strategy of "industrial unionism", which would contrast sharply with the class-collaborationist tactics of the AFL. The IWW, also known as the Wobblies, was founded in Chicago in 1905. Among its founders were legendary labour figure "Big Bill" Haywood, leader of the Western Federation of Miners; Eugene V Debs, the Socialist Party of America's presidential candidate in 1904; and Mary

Harris "Mother" Jones, the well-known Irish-American labour organiser.

The IWW was a huge step forward for the working class, and was unashamedly militant and anti-capitalist. Whereas the AFL had often gone along with racist sentiment in society—including a call for restrictions on immigration—the IWW preached working class unity and interracial solidarity. Leaflets were produced in multiple languages and open appeals were made for black workers to join them. In contrast to the AFL's refusal to make any serious effort to recruit women workers, the IWW boldly declared that women "cannot be driven back into the home...they are part of the army of Labour" (Kieran Allen, *The Politics of James Connolly*, 1990, p67).

And the union was unashamedly militant and anti-capitalist, declaring at its foundation, "The working class and the employing class have nothing in common. There can be no peace so long as hunger and want are found among millions of the working people and the few, who make up the employing class, have all the good things of life. Between these two classes a struggle must go on until the workers of the world organise as a class, take possession of the means of production, abolish the wage system, and live in harmony with the Earth... It is the historic mission of the working class to do away with capitalism. The army of production must be organised, not only for everyday struggle with capitalists, but also to carry on production when capitalism shall have been overthrown."

Connolly was immediately drawn to the Wobblies. He was attracted by their militancy, their advocacy of strike action and their uncompromising anti-capitalism. But he was also heavily influenced by the IWW's syndicalism, its strategy of organising "One Big Union" to confront the power of capital. Revolutionary syndicalism was based on the belief that the working class could build up economic control of society, industry by industry, ultimately laying the basis for a socialist reconstruction of society through a general strike. As Connolly put it himself, "Every fresh shop or factory organised under its banner is a fort wrenched from the control of the capitalist class and manned with the soldiers of the revolution to be held by them for the workers" (James Connolly, *Socialism Made Easy*, 1908).

There were a number of impressive strengths to the IWW strategy. Firstly, it eschewed the reformism and capitulation that were all too common in the labour movement, both in the US and internationally. Secondly, it placed a huge emphasis on the power of the working class itself, rather than on a small number of trade union leaders who would organise on their behalf. "Your union must be perfected," Connolly wrote, "until it embraces everyone who toils in the service of your employer, or as a unit in your industry" (James Connolly, *Socialism Made Easy*).

However, syndicalism was also hampered by a number of weaknesses. Firstly, the IWW believed that socialism could be created gradually, "industry by industry". As Connolly put it, this "was the swiftest, safest, and most peaceful" way to win socialism (James Connolly, *Socialism Made Easy*). This belief was based on the idea that capitalism itself had slowly grown within feudalism, taking over the economy and accumulating its economic strength as it went on. Syndicalism was premised on the idea that the working class could achieve socialism in a similar manner. However, historical experience tells us otherwise: the working class cannot simply accumulate its strength in the same mechanical way that the capitalist class accumulated its wealth. The strength of the working class is based on its militancy and solidarity. Certainly this accumulates in the heat of battle, but it can also suffer setbacks.

The IWW's own history illustrates this well. Between its founding in 1905 and its decline just over a decade later the Wobblies went from a membership of tens of thousands of the most militant workers to a few hundred. There was to be no incremental takeover of the economy.

Syndicalism also underestimated the ability of the ruling class to divide workers. Workers fought the system, but they could also be influenced by the right wing propaganda disseminated through state institutions and the mass media. As Marx put it, "The ideas of the ruling class are in every epoch the ruling ideas" (Karl Marx, *The German Ideology*, 1845). For that reason it was necessary to combine the industrial struggle with a struggle for a party that could organise the most militant minority of the class around revolutionary ideas.

Although Connolly was not opposed to the need for a socialist party, unlike some others in the IWW, his experience in the SLP led him to the conclusion that what was needed was a broad organisation involving both reformists and revolutionaries. This approach was no doubt superior to De Leon's sectarianism. And it was also true that revolutionaries should find as much common ground with reformists as possible, including seeking alliances with them. But ultimately, for revolutionary ideas to win they needed to be organised, a point that Connolly's life would ultimately demonstrate.

Despite these difficulties, Connolly's stay in the US was a fruitful one. He worked for a period as an organiser for the Wobblies in New York and spoke regularly on their platforms. He assisted in the presidential election campaign of Socialist Party candidate Eugene V Debs, joining the organisation after his break with the SLP. In 1907, with Elizabeth Gurley Flynn and others, he helped found the Irish Socialist Federation (ISF), an organisation of Irish-American workers whose aim was to: "assist the revolutionary working-class movement in Ireland...and to prepare them to co-operate with the workers of all other races, colours and nationalities in the emancipation of labour" (James Connolly, *Declaration of Principles of the Irish Socialist Federation*, 1908).

Connolly also kept up his writing and produced a pamphlet in 1908, *Socialism Made Easy*, that was based on the politics he learned in the IWW. It was a brilliant piece of work, written in a clear popular style, and a wonderful exposition of basic socialist positions. There could be no doubt about Connolly's revolutionary intentions in this period: "We would certainly confiscate the property of the capitalist class," he declared, "but we do not propose to rob anyone. On the contrary, we propose to establish honesty once and forever as the basis of our social relations. This Socialist movement is indeed worthy to be entitled The Great Anti-Theft Movement of the Twentieth Century." Connolly appealed to his readers to ignore those who would deride revolutionary politics as impractical: "Moral— Don't be 'practical' in politics. To be practical in that sense means that you have schooled yourself to think along the lines, and in the grooves those who rob you would desire you to think" (James Connolly, *The Workshop Talks*, 1909).

By the end of the decade, however, Connolly had grown weary of his stay in the US. In one letter he declared his "emigration to America as the great mistake of my life" (Lorcan Collins, *James Connolly: 16 Lives*, p166). Later, when discussing a possible return to Ireland with his wife Lillie, she said to him, "Think of all the misery we had there. How can you want to go back?" To which he replied, "I love Dublin, Lillie. I'd rather be poor there than a millionaire here." His mind was set and Connolly was on his way back to Ireland, arriving in Derry on 26 July 1910 (Nora Connolly O'Brien, *James Connolly: Portrait of a Rebel Father*, 1975, p109).

★ 6: LABOUR IN IRISH HISTORY

James Connolly was an activist, but he also understood the importance of ideas and theory. He spent much of his time reading, and was a great populariser of socialist ideas through his articles and pamphlets. There is no doubting that his greatest work was *Labour in Irish History*—an accessible account of Irish history written from a socialist perspective—published in 1910.

The book was over a decade in the making and had its origins in a series of articles written by Connolly in the *Workers' Republic*. Connolly was modest about his achievement, insisting that "abler pens" would have to provide a fuller analysis of Ireland in the future. Of course Connolly's work, like any work, has its limitations. The scope of the book, however, is considerable. This was a popular history from below written long before history from below had become a common term; a sharp, sprawling materialist account of the development of Irish society and the different class forces that helped shape it.

Connolly had no time for romantic Irish nationalist myths. There is no singular, undifferentiated Irish nation in his account, no notion of an unbroken thread of 700 years of struggle. "Irish history", according to Connolly, "has ever been written by the master class—in the interests of the master class" (James Connolly, *Labour in Irish History*, Bookmarks, 1987, p25). Connolly's aim was to reveal this underlying class dynamic and "to repair the deliberate neglect of the social question by our historians", who had treated the role of the working class and lower orders "with contempt when he remains passive and with derision, hatred and misrepresentation whenever he dares evince a desire to throw off the yoke of political and social servitude"(James Connolly, *Labour in Irish History*, p25).

Labour in Irish History was Connolly's attempt at a historical materialist account of Irish history, and he took as his starting point the Marxist notion that history and progress were the result of a struggle between contending classes. "Without this key to the meaning of events," wrote Connolly, "this clue to unravel the actions of 'great men', Irish history is but a welter of unrelated facts, a hopeless chaos of sporadic outbreaks... With this key all things become understandable" (James Connolly, *Labour in Irish History*, p166). Connolly's Marxism led him to the understanding that the Irish National Question was a social question: "The whole age-long fight of the Irish people against their oppressors resolves itself in the last analysis into a fight for the mastery of the means of life, the sources of production, in Ireland" (James Connolly, *Labour in Irish History*, p166).

Connolly was not afraid to deconstruct some of Irish nationalism's most famous heroes. The Jacobite Padraig Sarsfield is revealed by Connolly to be a coward who "enjoyed the privileges of robbing the Irish people" (James Connolly, *Labour in Irish History*, p34). Henry

Grattan, the famous Irish parliamentarian, represented the "spirit of the bourgeoisie incarnate", the rising Irish capitalist class who feared the working class "more than they feared the British government" (James Connolly, *Labour in Irish History*, pp63-65). Daniel O'Connell—the Irish nationalist and leader of the movement for Catholic Emancipation, often described as the "Great Liberator"— gets particularly rough treatment. Connolly condemns O'Connell as "the most bitter and unscrupulous enemy of trade unionism Ireland has yet produced", citing his opposition to the banning of child labour, and chastises the nationalist for sowing sectarian division in the country through his relationship with the Catholic Church (James Connolly, *Labour in Irish History*, p123).

Central to *Labour in Irish History* is Connolly's internationalism. He sought to place events into their global context—and in the process break from the kind of Irish exceptionalism that was all too common among politicians both then and now—by revealing how the great outbursts of struggle in Ireland chimed with the rhythm of the struggle elsewhere in the world. The United Irishmen of 1798 were, according to Connolly, "an Irish expression of the tendencies embodied in the first French Revolution". The Young Irelander Rebellion of 1848 "throbbed in sympathy with the democratic and social upheavals" across Europe, and Fenianism in the 1860s was an Irish expression of the same process that "produced the International Working Men's Association" led by Karl Marx (all quotes, James Connolly, *Labour in Irish History*, pp162-163). It follows, of course, that any future social upheaval in Ireland would be shaped by and have its fate tied to global events, even if its leaders refused to recognise this.

Connolly insisted that only the working class were the "incorruptible inheritors of the fight for freedom in Ireland". He also argued, however, that the struggle for independence and socialism could not be won by the lower orders if they aligned themselves with the Irish bourgeoisie or landowners. The Irish bourgeoisie, according to Connolly, were not to be trusted. Even if rhetorically they supported independence, in the end they had "a thousand economic strings in the shape of investments binding them to English capitalism as against every historical attachment drawing them towards Irish patriotism (James Connolly, *Labour in Irish History*, p24). A "union of classes" always led to disaster for those at the bottom of society, Connolly insisted. As he wrote elsewhere, "No amount of protestations could convince intelligent workers that the class which grinds them down to industrial slavery can, at the same time, be leading them forward to national liberty" (*Shan Van Vocht*, August 1897).

Much of *Labour in Irish History* is an extended argument with "advanced nationalists". Connolly wanted to win republicans to a socialist position. In doing so he occasionally exaggerated the socialist credentials of radical republicans in the past. The United Irishmen are described as the representatives of the "men of no property"; but this ignores the actual class basis of their leadership within Ulster's rising merchant class. Certainly, Wolfe Tone and his comrades were impressive revolutionaries, but they were *bourgeois revolutionaries*, akin to those who led the French Revolution, not socialist revolutionaries based in the working class. Fintan Lalor is described as "an apostle of Irish revolutionary socialism", but in reality his politics—though advanced for the time—were in step with those of bourgeois revolutionaries elsewhere; like them he was a defender of the rights of private property.

Connolly hoped to be able to win republicans to the left. In the main, this reflected the weakness of the socialist movement in Ireland and the desire to win the advanced elements of the much larger republican current to class politics. But it also represented a theoretical weakness on Connolly's part. His approach was based on two mistaken presumptions. Firstly, Connolly believed that the capitalist system was a British import and that the "Irish character" was "too difficult to press into respectable foreign moulds" (James Connolly, *Labour in Irish History*, p21). Socialism, according to this schema, would therefore be the natural progression for any genuine republican. The notion that capitalism is incompatible with the Irish character is, in a sense, no more rational than the notion that socialism is a foreign import. The long history of capitalism in Ireland should suffice as evidence that the Irish are no more or no less socialistic than any other nationality.

Secondly, Connolly believed that the development of Irish capitalism by nationalists or republicans was impossible in a global market already saturated with competitors. Republicans, he believed, would be forced to go down a socialist direction to truly liberate Ireland. Unfortunately, the trajectory of the republican movement after Connolly's death—and the experience of countless national liberation movements across the globe ever since—has disproved the notion that radical movements for independence automatically travel down the socialist road. On the contrary, there has been a long litany of betrayals as nationalist movements have made their peace with the system and became the managers of capitalism. Even a cursory glance at Irish history—both recent and over the past century and a half—turns up a long list of similar examples. His execution at the hands of the world's most powerful empire deprived Connolly of the benefit of learning from this experience.

None of this should take away from the tremendous contribution that *Labour in Irish History* made to a socialist understanding of the national question. And the pillars of Connolly's argument—that the working class are the key agents for change, that the rich should not be trusted and that any struggle for socialism has to take up the struggle against oppression, including national oppression—remain every bit as relevant today as when Connolly first formulated it. His rousing conclusion, calling for working class unity in Ireland, should remain our rallying cry today: "In their movement the North and South will again clasp hands, again will it be demonstrated, as in '98, that the pressure of a common exploitation can make enthusiastic rebels out of a Protestant working class; earnest champions of civil and religious liberty out of Catholics, and out of both a united social democracy" (James Connolly, *Labour in Irish History*, p167).

★ 7: CONNOLLY IN BELFAST

On 27 May 1911 James Connolly and his family moved to Belfast, settling in the Falls Road area of the city. Belfast was at this time an industrial powerhouse, with tens of thousands employed in its massive shipyards, engineering works and linen mills. The city was then, as now, deeply divided—its working class long scarred by the effects of sectarian enmity between Catholics and Protestants.

First appearances can, however, be deceptive: beneath this communal animosity was a rich history of trade unionism and working class militancy in the city. Just four years before Connolly's arrival, for example, Belfast had been the scene of a mighty industrial upheaval which saw thousands of dock workers, led by Connolly's frequent collaborator Big Jim Larkin, down tools in one of the biggest labour disputes in the city's history. The strike went down to bitter defeat but its reverberations were still being felt when Connolly arrived in Belfast.

Connolly became central to radical politics and trade unionism in Belfast almost as soon as he arrived. He joined the Irish Transport and General Workers Union (ITGWU), and with Larkin's support became its Ulster organiser. He was immediately in the thick of things, helping to recruit new members and leading a strike of

300 dockers for better pay and conditions (in sympathy with a strike happening simultaneously in Liverpool). Connolly's years of experience and energy were central to the strike. He spoke at nightly meetings at Custom House Steps and organised a solidarity demonstration through the centre of the city. Symbolic of his successful efforts in fighting for class unity in the strike was convincing members of Catholic and Protestant Orange bands to play together and merge into a new band, later called the Non-Sectarian Labour Band. The strike was a significant success and the dockers won a number of concessions.

Connolly's stature as a capable labour leader was quickly reinforced. In October of 1911 he was approached by a number of victimised women workers. They were employed in the local linen mills—where conditions for the overwhelmingly female workforce were harsh and pay abysmally low—who had been locked out by their employers for engaging in spontaneous strike action. The workers had had it up to their ears with the cruel treatment meted out by their bosses: they had been threatened with fines should they laugh, sing, talk or fix their hair during working hours. Their own union, the Textile Operatives Society, refused to support their action. But the linen workers found an ally in James Connolly, who urged them to set up a strike committee, helped them organise solidarity and spoke at their meetings, including one at St Mary's Hall attended by over 3,000 people.

The strike was solid, but the bosses refused to negotiate. The women returned to work following Connolly's advice, with one caveat: should one worker be reprimanded for singing then they should all sing; should one worker be reprimanded for talking then they should all talk; and if one worker walked out they all should walk out. Connolly conceded that the strike did not win much by way of material gain, but "measured in terms of increased self-respect," he wrote, "the gain has been immense" (Donal Nevin, *James Connolly: A Full Life*, p401).

Working class struggle was central to Connolly's activity in Belfast. He insisted, though, that it was necessary to combine this agitation with a wider political fight. During his stay in Belfast the question of Irish Home Rule again came to prominence when the Liberal government in London was forced to initiate a parliamentary bill to legislate for it. The Home Rule question was, according to Connolly, "the greatest asset in the hands of reaction in Ireland, the never-failing decoy to lure the workers into the bogs of religious hatreds and social stagnation" (*Forward*, 11 March 1911).

Despite these reservations he supported Home Rule for Ireland, arguing that the continuation of British rule in Ireland was central to maintaining division within the working class. "When election time rolls around," he wrote, "the smug representative of Orangeism will beat the big drum of 'saving the Union' before the working class voters, and with that discord in their ears they will be deaf to the cry of the helpless victims of capitalist oppression" (*Forward*, 11 March 1911).

This did not mean he was naive about the role of Irish nationalists. Connolly condemned the "Orange fanatic and the capitalist-minded Home Ruler" alike, heaping scorn on the "Irish home rule landlords using the green sunburst of Erin to cloak their rackrenting in the festering slums of our Irish towns" (*Forward*, 12 July 1913).

His criticism also extended to the more radical republicans, who he chastised for failing to fight for a republic that working class people, including those from a Protestant background, could have a stake in. "When the Sinn Féiner speaks to men who are fighting against low wages and tells them that the Sinn Féin body has promised lots of Irish labour at low wages to any foreign capitalist who wishes to establish in Ireland, what wonder if they come to believe that a change from Toryism to Sinn Féinism would simply be a change from the devil they do know to the devil they do not know!" (*Irish Nation*, 23 January 1909).

Connolly wanted to win supporters of Home Rule to a socialist position, to fight for a workers' republic that would end capitalist exploitation as well as British rule. When the Liberal government began to betray its nationalist allies by proposing the partition of Ireland, Connolly opposed it on principle. Partition would lead to a "carnival of reaction", he predicted, and would assist "the Home Rule and Orange capitalists and clerics to keep their rallying cries before the public as the political watchwords of the day" (*Forward*, 21 March 1914).

Not everyone on the left agreed with Connolly. He clashed with those who refused to support Home Rule and who acquiesced in the face of Loyalist reaction, most famously with William Walker, a veteran of the Belfast labour movement. Connolly condemned the "gas and water socialism" of Walker, accusing him of focusing exclusively on economic issues and evading the wider political questions. Connolly insisted that the menace of sectarianism—and organisations like the Orange Order which espoused it—could not be ignored. "A real Socialist movement cannot be built by temporising in front of the dying cause of Orange ascendancy", he insisted (*Forward*, 23 August 1913).

Connolly dismissed the notion that sectarianism arose out of immutable cultural differences, insisting it was the by-product of a colonial strategy of divide and rule. He warned that: "The Orange Order was not founded to safeguard religious freedom, but to deny religious freedom...in order to use religious zeal in the interests of the oppressive property rights of rackrenting landlords and sweating capitalists" (*Irish Worker*, 14 March 1914). None of this meant that Connolly was disparaging about the role of struggle over day-to-day issues. On the contrary, Connolly spent most of his time in Belfast—indeed most of his active political life—agitating around basic economic questions. Connolly's strategy, in sharp contrast to Walker's, was to combine a fight for Protestant and Catholic working class unity with principled opposition to sectarianism and imperialism.

To his credit, Connolly made every effort to put these words into practice. In the summer of 1912 sectarian tensions—egged on by the agitation of Unionist employers and politicians—were reaching boiling point. After skirmishes during the annual Twelfth of July Orange demonstrations, a wave of violence was unleashed against Catholics, some Protestant socialists and even some liberals who supported Home Rule. Sectarian mobs drove thousands of people out of work. Connolly was one of the few trade union figures in the city to attempt a response. He organised a meeting in the city centre against the expulsions, from which a demonstration was called, led by the Non-Sectarian Labour Band he had helped to organise. Unfortunately, very few trade unions followed Connolly's lead and most simply cowered in the face of Loyalist reaction. It was a disaster for working class politics in the city—the bitter fruits of a refusal to challenge sectarianism within the movement as Connolly had urged.

There is no doubt that Connolly's role in these disputes was exemplary. But his actions were those of an individual with a small following, and there was no organised socialist response to the crisis. Connolly was at this time a member of the Independent Labour Party—organised as a "broad church" rather than as a principled, revolutionary party, and he was often reduced to speaking in a personal capacity on questions like partition or sectarianism. Consequently, when he eventually left the city, no organised party was left behind that could fight for his revolutionary politics. This was a tragic shortfall and one that would leave the revolutionary left isolated in the tumultuous struggles that lay ahead.

★ 8: THE DUBLIN LOCKOUT

By 1913, Connolly's attention was turning from Belfast towards Dublin. The contrast between the two cities in this period could not have been greater. Whereas Belfast was in the throes of reaction and working class division, Dublin was gripped by "Larkinism" and a surge in militant trade union strike activity. These key developments formed the backdrop for one of Ireland's greatest industrial disputes—the Dublin Lockout.

Larkinism was an Irish version of the revolutionary syndicalist impulse then sweeping the globe, itself inspired by the 1905 Russian Revolution and which found its most prominent expression in the rise of the IWW. Instead of waiting for socialism to be delivered from on high by parliamentary representatives, Larkinism insisted that the working class could win it through their own self-activity.

Like the IWW that Connolly had worked with in America, Larkin's ITGWU was based around the idea of "One Big Union", discounting the need for a revolutionary party. Its militant industrial strategy—including the effective and widespread use of solidarity strike action among the working class—made it a force to be reckoned with. The union had its own paper, the *Irish Worker*, which promised its readers that it would be "a lamp to guide your feet in the dark hours of the impending struggle". The paper had a circulation of 20,000 and was widely read across the working class. Between 1910 and 1912 membership of the ITGWU rocketed from 4,000 to 22,000 members. This growth led to a succession of bitter struggles that won concessions from some of Dublin's biggest employers. The Irish capitalist class was terrified by the rise of Larkinism. The struggle about to commence would prove that their fears were well founded.

One company that refused to accede to the demands of the union was the Dublin Tram Company, owned by Ireland's most powerful capitalist, William Martin Murphy. Murphy—the owner of the *Irish Independent* newspaper—was intent on leading a capitalist counter-offensive against the rise of the ITGWU. He rallied his fellow employers to the cause. With the full backing of the British government—including the provision of police and troops to be used against strikers—Murphy began his attack on the union with a wholesale victimisation of suspected union members who worked for him.

The ITGWU responded by calling tram workers out on strike, resulting in the arrest of the union leadership. Connolly was sent to Dublin to help lead the strike. A mass rally was called for 31 August, but was banned by the state. Connolly joined Larkin in calling for resistance, an act that led to his arrest and sentencing to three months' imprisonment. The rally went ahead and the response of the state was swift and brutal. In what was to become known as Bloody Sunday, hundreds of workers were wounded when the police ran amok across Dublin. They beat people in the street with batons, attacked working class homes and assaulted men, women and even children. By the end of the weekend four people were dead. Believing that victory was at hand, the employers called a general lockout from 3 September in an effort to starve the ITGWU of support. By the end of the month nearly 25,000 workers were locked out of their jobs.

On 7 September Connolly began a hunger strike in protest at his imprisonment. The pressure worked and he was released. He resumed his role in the leadership of the strike after some rest and recuperation. The ITGWU was facing an increasingly violent backlash from the employers and the state. In October 1913 Connolly said from the window of Liberty Hall that he: "intended to organise and discipline a force to protect workers' meetings" (Lorcan Collins, *James Connolly: 16 Lives*, p219). This would eventually become the Irish Citizens Army (ICA), Europe's first workers' militia, organised to defend "the right to work and eat and live". According to Connolly: "it was resolved to create our own army to secure our rights, to protect our members, and to be a guarantee of our own free progress" (*Workers' Republic*, 30 October 1915).

Connolly was highly critical of those who refused to throw their lot behind the strike. When the ITGWU helped move the children of strikers to England so that they would not starve or suffer malnutrition, the Catholic Church attacked them, decrying the fact they had been sent to "godless" (that is, Protestant) England. The *Irish Catholic* newspaper, also owned by William Martin Murphy, described the strikers as "the foul reserves of the slums", and Catholic bishops issued a pastoral letter condemning the actions of the union. Some republicans supported the strike, including Pádraig Pearse. However,

Sinn Féin leader Arthur Griffith denounced Larkinism as an imported evil and even the Irish Republican Brotherhood (IRB) abstained from taking a position on the strike.

Central to the ITGWU's strategy was to build solidarity and spread the strike elsewhere. The Trades Council in London organised a mass rally in Trafalgar Square that was attended by thousands of English workers. Jim Larkin embarked on his "fiery cross crusade" tour across Britain, urging workers not to handle goods coming from Dublin as a way to win the dispute. The turnout at these meetings was massive and testified to the depths of solidarity among ordinary British workers for the strike in Ireland. Larkin's advice was followed by workers in a number of towns and cities, including Liverpool, Sheffield, Crewe, Birmingham and Derby. Hundreds of thousands of pounds was raised in solidarity with the strikers as well.

However, this fervour for action was not matched by the official trade union leadership. Rather than back the wildcat strike action spreading across Britain, many union leaders insisted that their members return to work. A special conference of the Trade Union Congress (TUC) was held on 9 December to discuss the lockout. Connolly and Larkin urged the TUC to officially support the boycott of goods coming from Dublin. If this course of action had been adopted, the strike could very well have won. Disgracefully, the resolution calling for such a strategy was overwhelmingly defeated.

Connolly was scathing in his assessment of the actions of the union leaders. "We asked for the isolation of the capitalists of Dublin, and for answer the leaders of the British Labour movement proceeded calmly to isolate the working class of Dublin... And so we Irish workers must go down into Hell, bow our backs to the lash of the slave driver, let our hearts be seared by the iron of his hatred, and instead of the sacramental wafer of brotherhood and common sacrifice, eat the dust of defeat and betrayal" (*Forward*, 9 February 1914).

The strikers were left isolated. Though the capitalist class had failed to defeat the ITGWU, the strike was undoubtedly defeated. Hundreds of ITGWU members were victimised and hundreds more were forced to disown the union in order get their jobs back. This meant that the Irish working class entered the turbulent years of the war after having suffered a catastrophic defeat. Despite this, a legacy of militant trade unionism had been laid in Dublin, something that would rise again during struggles later in the decade.

★ 9: THE WORLD AT WAR

The year 1914 was a particularly difficult one for James Connolly. In January the biggest and most bitterly fought working class upheaval that he had ever been involved with went down in defeat. And then in July 1914 the catastrophe for the working class, both in Ireland and across the world, deepened dramatically, as Europe's warring imperialist armies descended into one of the bloodiest conflicts in history. Millions of workers were to be starved, killed or wounded over the next four years in the name of capitalist competition. For a socialist like James Connolly, these were perhaps the darkest days of his life.

One further event greatly compounded this tragedy. The Second International—the body that linked labour and socialist parties the world over—capitulated in the face of the war. Connolly watched in horror as labour party after labour party—including the crown jewel of the Second International, the German Social Democratic Party—fell behind their own national armies or refused to oppose the war outright. Indeed, he had a taste of this himself in Ireland, when he was forced to resign from the Independent Labour Party (ILP) in Belfast after it refused to condemn the war. In fact, many of the ILP's leading figures, including Tom Johnson who would later become leader of the Irish Labour Party, were enthusiastic supporters of the war. The organisation effectively collapsed as a result, leaving Connolly without even the semblance of socialist organisation around him during the turbulent years ahead.

James Connolly, however, would not go down without a fight. "Conscription or no conscription," he proudly declared, "they will never get me or mine" (*Irish Worker*, 5 September 1914). Connolly was one of only a handful of socialists internationally who opposed the war, alongside figures such as Rosa Luxemburg and Karl Liebknecht in Germany, Eugene Debs in the US, Lenin and Trotsky in Russia and John McClean in Scotland. Connolly was clear that one could not support an imperialist conflict and continue claim to be a socialist: "War is ever the enemy of progress," he insisted. "It is only possible when humanity is stifled, when the common interests of the human race are denied" (*Irish Worker*, 14 November 1914).

In opposition to the stomach-churning jingoism prevailing across Europe, Connolly warned that the coming conflict would devastate humanity, that women would "suffer most by this foreign war" and that the working class everywhere would pay a heavy price as the cannon-fodder for the capitalist class. "Civilisation is being destroyed before our eyes," he wrote presciently; "the results of generations of propaganda and patient heroic plodding and self-sacrifice are being blown into annihilation from a hundred cannon mouths; thousands of comrades with whose souls we have lived in fraternal communion are about to be done to death...this war appears to me as the most fearful crime of the centuries. In it the working class are to be sacrificed that a small clique of rulers and armament makers may sate their lust for power and their greed for wealth" (*Forward*, 15 August 1914).

Connolly was deeply disturbed about the impact that the war—and the subsequent capitulation by the Second International—would have on the working class movement. "What becomes of all our resolutions," he asked, "all our protests of fraternisation; all our threats of general strikes; all our carefully-built machinery of internationalism; all our hopes for the future? Were they all as sound and fury, signifying nothing?" (*Forward*, 15 August 1914).

Connolly raged against "the greatest of internationalists" who had become "raving jingoes howling for the blood of every rival of the British capitalist class". He understood that internationalism and solidarity among the working class of different countries were key to the victory of socialism and worried that the stance of the Second International might severely weaken prospects for solidarity in the future: "When the German artilleryman, a socialist serving in the German army of invasion, sends a shell into the ranks of the French army, blowing off their heads; tearing out their bowels, and mangling the limbs of dozens of socialist comrades in that force, will the fact that he, before leaving for the front 'demonstrated' against the war be of any value to the widows and orphans made by the shell he sent upon its mission of murder? Or, when the French rifleman pours his murderous rifle fire into the ranks of the German line of attack, will he be able to derive any comfort from the probability that his bullets are murdering or maiming comrades who last year joined in thundering 'hochs' and cheers of greeting to the eloquent Jaurès, when in Berlin he pleaded for international solidarity?" (*Forward*, 15 August 1914).

Connolly attempted to agitate against the war. He played a role in launching the Irish Neutrality League, which organised campaigns against enlistment and sought to keep Ireland out of the conflict. And he worked though the ITGWU to organise strikes for wage rises in the face of pro-war budgets. Despite the surge in jingoism then pervading Ireland, Connolly was not afraid to put himself in the firing line in order to oppose the war. When H H Asquith, the Liberal Prime Minister of Britain, came to address a recruitment rally in Mansion House in Dublin, the Dublin Trades Council and the ITGWU organised an anti-war rally against it. Connolly, Larkin and Constance Markievicz spoke, flanked by members of the ICA armed with rifles for protection.

Connolly is famously associated with the slogan "We serve neither King nor Kaiser", which adorned both the *Irish Worker* newspaper that he edited and the iconic banner that was flown from Liberty Hall for a period. In truth, Connolly's position was not always so clear cut. There is no doubting that his opposition to the war was driven by his deeply held internationalism and anti-imperialism: "the socialist of another country is a fellow-patriot as the capitalist of my own country is a natural enemy" (*Forward*, 15 August 1914). At times, however, Connolly's insistence that "the main enemy is at home" could stray into equivocation on the reactionary nature of German imperialism. He once wrote, for example, that: "the German Empire is a homogeneous Empire of self-governing peoples" that contained "in germ more of the possibilities of freedom and civilisation [than the British Empire]" (*Workers' Republic*, 18 March 1916).

Despite these shortcomings, Connolly's opposition to the war was immeasurably better than those in the Second International who fell in behind their own ruling classes. The descent into war and the defeats suffered by the Irish labour movement which had preceded it created a sense of deep pessimism, maybe even desperation on Connolly's part. Throughout this, however, he hoped that the labour movement could revive itself and rise again to defeat imperialism: "Should the working class of Europe, rather than slaughter each other for the benefit of kings and financiers, proceed tomorrow to erect barricades all over Europe, to break up bridges and destroy the transport service that war might be abolished, we should be perfectly justified in following such a glorious example and contributing our aid to the final dethronement of the vulture classes that rule and rob the world" (*Irish Worker*, 8 August 1914).

"A great continental uprising of the working class", wrote Connolly, "would stop the war." This perspective was eventually proven correct and the war ended after revolutions in Russia and Germany. But Connolly did not live to see these uprisings come to fruition. In those dark days of war that formed the backdrop for his final years, the prospects for such an upheaval must have seemed bleak, and this inevitably shaped his course of action. It is to Connolly's credit that despite such difficult circumstances he refused to succumb to pessimism. "Ireland may yet set the torch to a European conflagration," he wrote, "that will not expire until the last throne and the last capitalist bond and debenture will be shrivelled on the funeral pyre of the last war lord" (*Irish Worker*, 8 August 1914). The road to the Easter Rising was set.

★ 10: THE EASTER REBELLION OF 1916

Understandably, the period of labour's immiseration after the defeat of the lockout combined with the collapse of the broader international socialist movement continued to afflict Connolly with a deep sense of political pessimism. But it also sparked an urgent recognition that something needed to be done, that somewhere a blow had to be struck against the madness.

Connolly did not have a credible revolutionary political organisation around him that he might mobilise to begin to turn the tide. Instead he looked to the ICA as a means to further the revolutionary cause. At this point the ICA was significantly depleted from its height during the lockout, with some former members so desperate that they enlisted in the British ranks. When the Irish Volunteers split with the nationalist John Redmond over support for the war, Connolly saw an opportunity to deepen alliances with republican forces and to strike a blow against empire. Through the ICA he agitated publicly for insurrection, an approach that was considered highly dangerous by his republican allies, who were more wedded to conspiratorial methods.

There are many myths about the Easter Rising. Perhaps the most oft repeated is that those involved in the action were engaged in a "blood sacrifice"—that they willingly, even enthusiastically, went out to die for a glorious but hopeless cause. This was plainly not the case. Had all gone to plan, the Rising had a reasonable chance of success. Owing to the escalating war in mainland Europe, there were relatively few British troops stationed in Ireland at this time; with only 6,000 combat troops and 9,500 Royal Irish Constabulary scattered across the length and breadth of the country. The rebels hoped to have as many as 16,000 Irish volunteers involved in a plan that called for simultaneous risings across the country. The insurgents had organised and were expecting the arrival of thousands of new weapons, and detailed military plans had been drawn up. These were hardly the acts of people looking forward to martyrdom.

Connolly threw himself into serious planning for the insurrection. The ITGWU headquarters in Dublin at Liberty Hall became one of the main planning centres, with guns and ammunition stored there. Connolly's objective was to strike a serious blow against the British Empire; he had always believed that a revolutionary upheaval in Ireland could be the spark that lit the revolution across Europe. The ICA was a very small force, however, numbering not more than a few hundred volunteers. They were greatly outnumbered by the larger republican forces. That said, Connolly had not simply collapsed into nationalism, and he was clear all through the period of preparation that he was fighting for the cause of the working class. "We are out for Ireland for the Irish," he confirmed. "But who are the Irish? Not the rack-renting, slum-owning landlord;

not the sweating, profit-grinding capitalist; not the sleek and oily lawyer; not the prostitute pressman—the hired liars of the enemy. Not these are the Irish upon whom the future depends. Not these, but the Irish working class, the only secure foundation upon which a free nation can be reared" (*Workers' Republic*, 8 April 1916).

It is often presumed that Connolly was a reluctant participant in the Rising, and among republicans there is a myth that he was forcibly co-opted into taking part. Recollections of some of those involved in the event—archived at the Bureau of Military History in Dublin—suggest, instead, that he was the most ardent proponent of action. Throughout the period running up to Easter 1916 Connolly agitated and argued with republicans for an insurrection. The long and sorry history of botched or failed uprisings in Irish history no doubt weighed heavily on his mind.

Despite extensive preparation, prospects for the Rising were significantly damaged by two developments. Firstly, the German ship, the *Aud*, was spotted by British naval forces off the coast of Cork, and the ship's crew sank it to prevent the capture of its arms, resulting in the loss of 20,000 rifles and a million rounds of ammunition that were to be used in the Rising.

Secondly, the loss of the *Aud* reinforced the sentiment among more cautious IRB leaders—grouped around Eoin MacNeill and Bulmer Hobson—that the Rising should be called off completely. MacNeill issued a countermanding order instructing volunteers not to involve themselves in military manoeuvres on Easter Sunday. The Rising was delayed by a day, but Connolly, Pearse and the rest of the leadership decided to go ahead. Even if they had not, it is likely that the British would soon have rounded them up anyway, as soon as they got wind of the plans. After this series of mishaps and internal disputes, however, the rebellion would go ahead with far fewer numbers, and with the element of surprise in doubt.

In the end approximately 1,300 insurgents, including 152 from Connolly's ICA, took part in the Rising—far fewer than had been originally intended. It was not only men that were involved in the rebellion, as is sometimes assumed; up to 100 women are estimated to have taken part in the Rising, many of them members of the republican organisation Cumann na mBan.

The rebels occupied a number of key buildings in Dublin, including the General Post Office (GPO), which became their de facto headquarters; the Four Courts, the centre of the Irish legal establishment; Boland's Mill; Jacob's Biscuit Factory; the South Dublin Union Hospital complex; and the Distillery at Marrowbone Lane. At a few minutes past noon on Easter Monday, 24 April 1916, Pádraig Pearse, flanked by Connolly, emerged from the GPO in Dublin and read out a proclamation that declared the birth of the Irish Republic. The proclamation guaranteed "religious and civil liberty, equal rights and equal opportunities of all its citizens" and vowed to "[cherish] all the children of the nation equally".

The British political and military establishment in Ireland were caught off guard by the Rising, and Connolly was right in the thick of the action. Those who survived recalled that he held no pretentions about his role, playing a full part in the fighting throughout. He paid the price for his commitment and his active leadership with two serious wounds—a bullet through his shoulder and a second that shattered his lower leg. As the week progressed the British military became increasingly stronger, capturing strategic positions in intense street fighting while their warships moored in the Liffey hurled artillery into the dense streets of urban Dublin. Thousands of reinforcements were drafted in, overwhelming the rebels and outgunning them. Eventually the leadership of the Rising had no choice but to surrender.

What, then, was the significance of the Easter Rising? Perhaps the best assessment came not from within Ireland, but from the Russian revolutionary Lenin. He defended the Rising and was scornful of those who saw it as a hopeless military adventure: "Whoever expects a 'pure' social revolution will never live to see it. Such a person pays lip-service to revolution without understanding what revolution is." However, Lenin added that it was regrettable that the Rising happened before a revolutionary reaction against the war had generated outbreaks elsewhere: "It is the misfortune of the Irish that they rose prematurely, before the European revolt of the proletariat had had time to mature" (V I Lenin, *The Discussion On Self-Determination Summed Up*, 1916). This prognosis was proved correct and within a few years Ireland, and indeed much of Europe, was gripped by revolutionary upheaval. Sadly, Connolly would not live to see this.

The scale of the repression meted out by the British— including the summary execution of 16 of the Rising's leaders and the internment of 3,600 people—generated a wave of sympathy throughout Irish society. William Martin Murphy's right wing *Irish Independent* led the calls for Connolly to be put to the firing squad, in part no doubt in revenge for his leading role in the 1913 Lockout.

Connolly's wife Lillie and his eldest daughter Nora were summoned late at night to Dublin Castle, where the wounded man was being kept under armed guard. The news was not good. "Well, Lillie. I suppose you know what this means," Connolly said poignantly. Lillie immediately knew his fate had been decided: "It's not that—it's not that," she wailed, "your beautiful life, James. Your beautiful life." There was nothing that could be done. "Hasn't it been a full life" he asked his wife in an effort to comfort her "and isn't this a good end?" (Lorcan Collins, *James Connolly: 16 Lives*, pp305-306).

It would be the final time they ever laid eyes on each other. On 12 May 1916 James Connolly was brought to Kilmainham Gaol. Blindfolded and clad only in his pyjamas, unable to stand due to the severity of his wounds, Ireland's most important socialist thinker and activist was tied to a chair. The firing squad awaited him. A remarkable life was over.

★ 11: CONCLUSION

Where oh where is our James Connolly?" So goes the famous Irish ballad, lamenting the loss of one of the finest socialists ever to have lived. It was a sentiment shared across Ireland long before those words were ever written. The death of James Connolly was a terrible blow to the workers' movement and to socialists here and the world over.

Lenin's judgment that the Easter Rising had come too early, before the European reaction against the barbarism of the First World War had matured, was proven correct. Within 18 months the situation had changed dramatically: Russia was gripped by a revolutionary upsurge, overthrowing the Tsarist regime and, in October, leading to a socialist revolution. The rest of Europe soon followed suit, with the working class asserting its power in country after country—Hungary and the German province of Bavaria saw the creation of short-lived soviet republics, and left-led uprisings occurred in Berlin and Vienna. Even in those countries where events fell short of a revolutionary challenge for power, such as Italy or Britain, wave after wave of industrial unrest and huge general strikes would shape the contours of politics. As Connolly had foreseen, it was workers' revolution that brought an end to war between the Great Powers.

Ireland was not immune to this revolutionary fervour. A combination of guerrilla war organised by a resurgent republican movement and a massive campaign of strikes and civil disobedience in which labour played a leading role rocked British rule in Ireland. The working class was right at the heart of the Irish Revolution. On 23 April 1918 a general strike was organised against conscription. The *Irish Times* described it "as the day on which Irish Labour realised its strength". In 1919 the spectre of working class unity re-emerged in Belfast during a general strike demanding the introduction of the 42-hour working week. And in Limerick a "soviet" was formed—inspired by the workers' councils established during Russia's revolutionary upsurge—which ran the city from 15 to 27 April 1919, printing its own currency and organising the city's food supply.

The Irish Revolution was not to end in the victorious march of socialism, as Connolly had hoped. The working class was left without a political expression during these tumultuous years, without an organised force that could draw its best fighters together around a fight for revolutionary socialism. Connolly had left a brilliant legacy, but he left no party behind that could fight for his ideas after his death. Instead nationalist forces made their peace with the British, acceding to a partitioned Ireland, and creating a conservative Catholic state in the 26 counties. In the North unionist forces set about consolidating their power, laying the foundations for a sectarian state that would protect capitalist interests to the detriment of the working class, and particularly its Catholic minority. Connolly warned that such a scenario would lead to a carnival of reaction, and right he was: the two conservative states that still survive in Ireland today are a product of this counter-revolution.

The ghost of James Connolly continues to haunt the Irish establishment. Try as they might, the radical legacy that he left behind cannot be completely extinguished. The true story of his life remains an embarrassment to a Southern conservative elite which would rather forget that one of their most famous heroes was a revolutionary Marxist. Nor do Connolly's life and legacy sit well with the Orange and Green forces that today run the North of Ireland; his call for Catholic and Protestant workers to unite in a fight against capitalism and sectarianism contrasts sharply with a political setup that portrays communal difference as inevitable.

Nevertheless, thousands of people across Ireland and the world are wondering anew about James Connolly. As part of this process a new generation will have to excavate his legacy from beneath the rubble of establishment distortion, and rediscover his extraordinary contributions to the struggle for a more equal world. He made mistakes, of course, but he did so in the thick of the struggle, and always on the side of the workers and the oppressed. All things considered, James Connolly has few equals in Irish history; as comfortable in the realm of ideas as he was in the thick of action, outstanding as a thinker, fighter and agitator. James Connolly was a revolutionary to the end. And that is his true epitaph.

FURTHER READING

There are a number of biographies of James Connolly. Donal Nevin's
James Connolly: A Full Life (Gill & Macmillan, 2006) is the most
comprehensive, Lorcan Collins *James Connolly: 16 Lives* (O'Brien's
Press, 2012) is the most readable, and Kieran Allen's *The Politics of
James Connolly* (Pluto Press, 1990) the most thoroughgoing analysis
of Connolly's politics. The best way to access Connolly's own writings
is through the Marxist Internet Archive at www.marxists.org. Shaun
Harkin's *A James Connolly Reader* (Haymarket, 2016) is an excellent
collection as well.

More Bookmarks Rebel's Guides

Available from Bookmarks, the socialist bookshop
1 Bloomsbury Street, London WC1B 3QE
info@bookmarksbookshop.co.uk
bookmarksbookshop.co.uk
020 7637 1848

A REBEL'S GUIDE TO MARX
Mike Gonzalez
£3
This concise guide offers an introduction to Marx's ideas, from his analysis of what drives corporate globalisation to his discussion of how human liberation can be achieved.

A REBEL'S GUIDE TO LENIN
Ian Birchall
£3
A pocket guide to the real Lenin. It shows his methods and motivations in attempting to create a world in which production was to be for human need rather than profit.

A REBEL'S GUIDE TO GRAMSCI
Chris Bambery
£3
Antonio Gramsci was one of the most remarkable Marxists of the 20th century. This introduction to his life and world highlights how much his ideas still have to offer us today.

SEXISM AND THE SYSTEM:
A REBEL'S GUIDE TO WOMEN'S LIBERATION
Judith Orr
£3
We are told that women are now equal to men.
This socialist case for women's liberation argues
why winning the battle means changing the world.

A REBEL'S GUIDE TO TROTSKY
Esme Choonara
£3
Many people have heard the name, but how
many know about Leon Trotsky's life or ideas?
He was a central figure in the decisive event of
the 20th century, the Russian Revolution of 1917.

A REBEL'S GUIDE TO ROSA LUXEMBURG
Sally Campbell
£3
Rosa Luxemburg was one of the key leaders of
the German revolutionary left until her murder
in 1919 at the height of the attempted revolution.
She was an orator, teacher and leader.

A REBEL'S GUIDE TO ELEANOR MARX
Siobhan Brown
£3
Eleanor Marx was a passionate champion of the
oppressed who linked everyday struggles to the
big picture. This guide places her back alongside
other revolutionary leaders, where she belongs.

Scene in the General
just before

Easte